HOW THEY
LIVED

A NORMAN BARON

MIRIAM MOSS

Illustrated by
Mark Bergin

HOW THEY LIVED

Editor: Amanda Earl

First published in 1987 by
Wayland (Publishers) Limited
61 Western Road, Hove
East Sussex BN3 1JD, England

© Copyright 1987 Wayland (Publishers) Limited
British Library Cataloguing in Publication Data
Moss, Miriam
A Norman baron. – (How they lived).
1. Normans – England – History – Juvenile literature
2. Great Britain – History –
Norman period, 1066–1154 – Juvenile literature
I. Title   II. Bergin, Mark   III. Series
942.02   DA195

ISBN 0 85078 673 8

Typeset by Kalligraphics Limited, Redhill, Surrey
Printed and bound in Belgium by Casterman S.A.

CONTENTS

THE KING'S VISIT

Darkness was falling over the great hall of the baron's castle. A kitchen boy placed rushes dipped in mutton fat into the iron holders on the walls and lit them. They flickered in the cold draught as the baron entered with his knights. They had been hunting in the deep forests surrounding the castle.

The baron's wife ordered fresh rushes to be spread over the stone floor. Servants scurried excitedly here and there. They were preparing for William the Conqueror's visit.

In January 1066, Edward the Confessor, King of England, died. His cousin, William Duke of Normandy, claimed the English throne. But, an English nobleman, Harold Godwinson, had himself crowned king, even

A scene from the Bayeux Tapestry, showing Harold's army under attack at the Battle of Hastings in 1066.

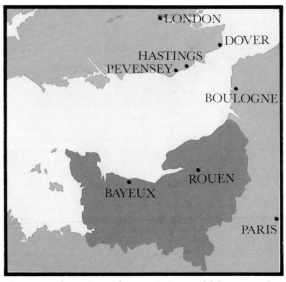

A map showing the position of Normandy.

though he had once sworn to support William's claim to the throne.

William of Normandy gathered an army in France. In September 1066 he landed his longships, carrying about 6,000 men, at Pevensey Bay in Sussex. William and Harold's armies met at Hastings on 14 October. The battle raged all day. But by late afternoon Harold lay dead and his English army was defeated. William the Conqueror was crowned King of England on Christmas Day, 1066, in Westminster Abbey. Norman kings continued to rule England until 1154.

5

KINGS, BARONS AND SERFS

After conquering England, William kept about a quarter of the land for himself and gave a quarter to the Church. The rest of the land he gave to the Norman barons who helped him conquer England. In return, the barons swore to be loyal to the king and provide soldiers for his army.

Most of the barons had enough land to give some of it to their knights. Each area of land was known as a 'manor'. A baron or knight who owned a manor was called 'Lord of the Manor'.

The lord divided some of the land attached to the manor into two or three large open fields. He then divided the fields into strips and rented it to the villagers. The strips of land were shared fairly so that no one held all the good land. Villagers paid for the rent of this land in a number of ways. Rich families in the village paid a rent of money, while

A typical Norman manor, showing the castle, local church, villagers' homes and the large open fields.

freemen paid the lord with some of the produce that they grew.

Villeins were serfs, forced to live on the manor in which they were born. They paid for the land they used by working part of the week in the lord's own fields. A villein holding 60 strips of land would have to work about 3 days a week for his lord, while a villein holding 20 strips worked only 1 day for his lord.

Those who farmed on the lord's land were watched over by the lord's reeve. The baron also had a steward, a bailiff and a clerk to help him manage the land. Such men were very important if the baron had more than one manor.

The steward looked after the most pressing business on the manor, while the bailiff took care of the everyday running of the village. He collected the village 'tithes' of corn, hens and hay for the baron.

In Norman times, any man who rented or was given land promised to serve the person who gave it to him. Therefore, the farmers and villeins supported and served the baron, who in turn supported the king. This system of government was known as the 'feudal system'.

NORMAN CASTLES

The Norman barons knew they were hated by the English, and in constant danger of attack, so they built castles to protect themselves.

The first castles were made of wood and earth, taking only a couple of weeks to build. They were known as motte and bailey castles. The 'motte' was a circular mound of earth, which had a square wooden tower or 'keep' on top of it. The flat area below the great mound was surrounded by a high wooden fence. This was called the 'bailey'. Some castles had an inner and an outer bailey, as well as a moat to put off attackers!

Inside the bailey it was something like a small village, but in times of danger everybody gathered in the

A view of a Norman castle. The inner and outer bailey, as well as the moat, provided protection from enemies.

keep, as it was the safest place to be. Motte and bailey castles were easily set on fire by the enemy, so gradually Norman barons replaced them with stronger stone castles.

Stone castles often took many years to build and involved as many as 2,000 craftsmen and builders. They were like the earlier wooden castles, with a keep, high surrounding walls and a moat, but they had much deeper foundations and the

Most castle keeps had a chapel. This is the chapel inside the keep of Dover Castle in Kent.

Rochester Castle with its strong stone walls is a fine example of an existing Norman keep.

walls were much more solid.

The entrance was the weakest part of a Norman castle, so a strong gatehouse, called a 'barbican', was built to protect it. The barbican contained a drawbridge to span the moat, which could be easily raised in times of danger to stop the enemy crossing it. A huge iron grating, called a 'portcullis' could also be lowered to bar the entrance to the castle.

The huge stone keep was the place where all the weapons and armour was stored, and where some of the people lived.

9

LIVING IN A CASTLE

Norman castles must have been very uncomfortable to live in. In summer, they were probably damp, dark and cold, but in winter they must have been freezing. There were no windows to let any light in, just narrow slits in the stone. These slits were called 'wind's eyes' from which we get the word window today. Arrows could be fired from them in times of danger.

The keep was the main part of the castle, and its floors were covered in dry reeds which were left until they became rotten and smelly. All rubbish was thrown into an open pit called a 'midden', where it just decayed. The toilets were tiny rooms sticking out from the walls of the keep. They emptied straight into the castle's moat, which must have become very unhygenic after a time. There were no bathrooms as people rarely washed.

The most important part of the keep was the great hall. It was a huge, dark, smoky place. A great log fire was usually kept alight, and this provided some warmth, but there were no proper chimneys, so all the smoke just lingered in the room. Everybody gathered here to eat. Many people actually slept in this room too, huddled on benches, or just lying on the cold floor, wrapped in their cloaks.

The baron and his family had special living quarters at the top of the keep, known as the solar. Craftsmen, such as saddlers, shoemakers and stonemasons also made their home in the keep.

The keep had an armoury, in the basement. This was where all the weapons and armour were safely kept in case of attack, or in the event of a war breaking out. The keep had a well, which provided drinking water. This was very important, if the castle was ever under siege. On the lower level of the keep there were many storerooms, which were kept as well stocked as possible with food, ale and wine.

A Norman castle was many things – it was a home, a barracks, a refuge for villagers in danger, and a prison for law-breakers!

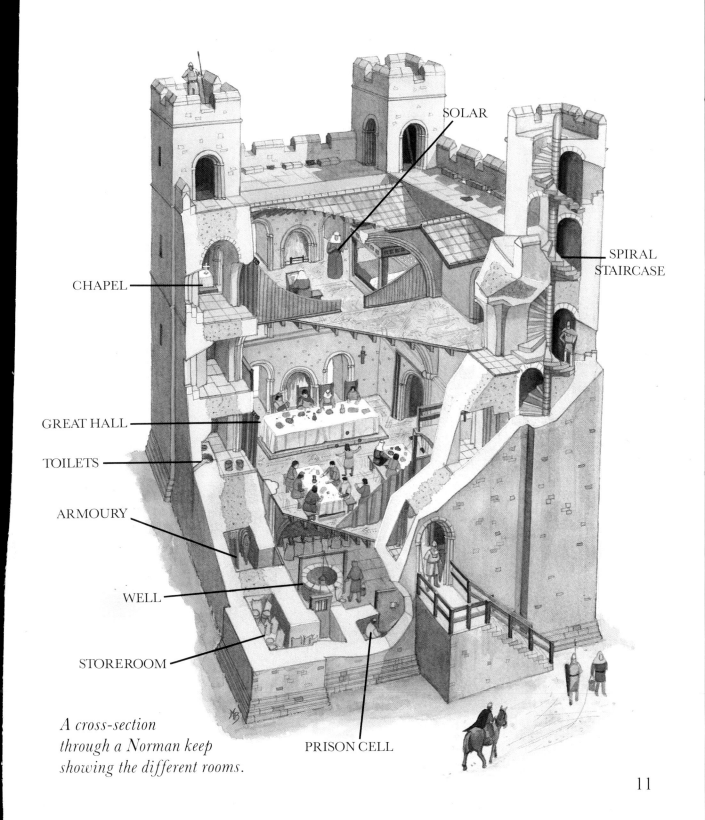

SOLAR

SPIRAL
STAIRCASE

CHAPEL

GREAT HALL

TOILETS

ARMOURY

WELL

STOREROOM

PRISON CELL

*A cross-section
through a Norman keep
showing the different rooms.*

11

FEASTING

The main meal in a Norman castle was eaten between 10am and 11am, and a light supper was served at about 5pm. The baron, his family and guests sat at a table on a platform at one end of the great hall. A large number of cooks worked hard in the great kitchens preparing the food. Servants carried the steaming-hot food to the tables. Dogs and beggars wandered about looking for scraps, while jugglers and minstrels entertained.

Only the rich barons had their own cups, plates and knives. Eating was a messy business and people usually washed their hands at the beginning and end of each meal. Most of the food was very simple. The soldiers used chunks of rough bread as plates and ate salted beef. They drank ale from shared cups. Only the baron and his family enjoyed food like roast|songbirds, seagulls and meat pies. Instead of ale, they preferred to drink wine.

In winter, food became very scarce and only the baron had meat. Even then, not much of the meat was fresh. Most was salted to keep it from rotting. Sometimes the baron and his guests went hunting and brought back venison and partridge to eat. Very few vegetables were grown in England at this time. There were no cabbages or potatoes, but beans and peas were eaten, as well as fruit and nuts. At the end of each meal the servants tipped the leftover food, bones and fruit on to the floor where the dogs fought over it or it was left to rot along with the rushes.

Cooks worked hard in the kitchens preparing the food. Meat was cooked on a large spit and roasted over a fire.

Right *Everybody met in the great hall for a feast.*

CLOTHES AND HAIRSTYLES

The Norman baron wore a 'sherte' over which he wore a tunic and an overtunic. This was often edged with fur and tied with a large leather belt. It must have been bitterly cold in the castle in winter, so then he would also have worn a mantle and over it a heavy cloak. He wore breeches and thick 'hose' (stockings) covered his legs. On his feet he wore soft

A Norman baron and his family in everyday clothes. They were made from fine materials like silk and linen.

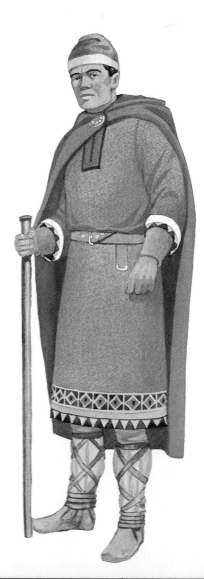

Serfs wore plain clothes of rough wool and canvas. It must have been difficult to work in long clothes like these.

leather shoes. These had pointed toes stuffed with wool and were sometimes brightly coloured. He wore his hair very short and often wore a hat indoors and outdoors, not even taking it off to eat!

The baron's wife wore an undergarment called a chemise. She wore hose and pointed narrow shoes and a long gown pulled in at the waist with a belt. Some gowns were made with tightly laced bodices. She wore a wimple over her head, covering her long plaited hair. The mantle she wore was held in place by cords across the front. Children dressed as their parents did but the girls wore their hair loose.

Rich barons' clothes were made of linen, fur and silk. The barons' serfs made their own simple clothes from canvas, skins and rough wool. They wore a tunic, a hood, cross-gartered trousers and the more fortunate wore wooden clogs or leather boots.

On special occasions, such as a meeting with King William, the baron wore more elaborate clothes.

15

FAMILY LIFE

The baron and his wife were very strict with their children. They decided who the children would marry, and girls often married at 14 or even before. A girl agreed to marry a man at a meeting called a 'betrothal', which was considered almost as important as the marriage ceremony. A wife's first duty was to give her husband male heirs! She also had to be good at running the castle when her husband was away fighting.

When children reached the age of 7 they were expected to behave like little adults. Boys had to put up with

The 'solar' was where the baron and his family lived. It was here that the baron's wife carried out most of her day-to-day business.

The baron's wife and daughters also spent their time spinning and weaving in the solar.

pheasants with a stone bow, which shot pebbles from a sling.

In Norman England many people died when they were very young. Many children died in infancy or before reaching the age of 10. Because of diseases and little knowledge of medicine, few people lived beyond the age of 30.

Little was known about medicine in Norman times, although herbal remedies, like the one described in this book, were very common.

rough treatment without complaint and girls had to learn how to behave like dignified ladies.

The baron and his wife slept in a private room called the 'solar'. This was the centre of the baron's family life. The family spent time here during the day. After morning prayers, at sunrise, the lady and her daughters would go to the solar to spin, do needlework or make medicines from herbs. In the afternoons the children often went hunting in the woods with the head huntsman. Here, under the watchful eyes of a few knights as bodyguards, the children would learn to shoot

EDUCATION AND LANGUAGE

Most barons' sons were sent to live in a neighbouring baron's castle at the age of 7. They served as pages to the baron, learning how a member of the upper classes had to behave. They were also taught how to fight on horseback, and how to use a sword and lance. In some castles, boys learned to read and write in Latin, but many barons' sons learned little more than how to write their name.

Girls were often better educated than their brothers as they did not spend so much time learning to fight and hunt. They were taught at

Barons' sons were usually sent away to another castle to learn about fighting, hunting and jousting.

home by teachers or in convents.

Some younger sons were sent to cathedrals or monasteries to become priests or monks. Cathedrals and monasteries were the centres of learning at this time. Every centre had its own form of handwriting. The boys wrote in ink with a quill pen. The parchment they wrote on could be sponged clean and re-used. Most teachers believed in harsh punishment. For any slight mistake, the master would beat the pupil across the shoulders with a stout cane.

The old English language spoken in England before the Norman invasion started to change as Norman-French words came into the language. Norman barons who spoke French gradually began to speak English, but still used thousands of Norman-French words. Many such words are still used today – 'baron', 'servant', 'messenger' and 'feast'.

Younger sons often became monks.

SPORTS

Barons and knights in Norman England spent much of their time in the countryside, hunting with bows and arrows on horseback. They hunted wild boar, wolves, deer, foxes and hares. Hunting gave the barons and knights exercise and riding practice that was useful in time of war. It also provided food for those back at home. They hunted using hawks and falcons too, which killed smaller birds in mid-flight.

Serfs often poached off the baron's land, shooting the game with bows and arrows and snaring rabbits and hares. If they were caught, they would be severely punished.

The barons encouraged their soldiers to keep well practiced in using their bows, and archery competitions were often held. In some villages there were special places for archery practice. A mound of earth, covered in grass was marked with

Barons and their knights spent much of the time hunting.

20

circles to act as a target.

In winter if the baron's pond froze over the villagers would skate on it using skates made from animal bones. A sort of football was played by the baron's serfs too. Sometimes the goals were in different villages so the pitch was about 5 to 6 kilometres long! The baron's children played football and a kind of cricket using a curved stick called a cryc. They also played hockey, skittles and a game similar to golf.

The barons and knights enjoyed taking part in tournaments. Wooden grandstands were put up so the barons and their ladies could sit and watch. There would be colourful banners flying and great excitement amongst the crowd. Two groups of heavily armed knights fought mock battles. Many knights were badly injured or killed by the thundering hooves of the huge warhorses. Barons and knights also took part in individual jousting tournaments. The aim was to unhorse the charging opponent with a long lance.

OTHER ENTERTAINMENTS

The bands of travelling minstrels that visited the baron's castle were very popular entertainers. They sang songs about saints or about the brave deeds of knights. The baron and his family always welcomed these entertainers as they brought the latest news and gossip from other parts of the land. Some sang comic songs accompanied by a lute or bagpipes.

These minstrels were sometimes joined by jugglers, contortionists or ropewalkers, or by performers who used bears and monkeys to do tricks.

Minstrels were popular entertainers.

The baron also enjoyed watching the wandering actors who travelled through the countryside performing 'miracle' plays. These plays were based on a story from the Bible or the life of a saint.

Sometimes Norman barons watched very cruel entertainments like cock fighting or bull or bear baiting. There were also wrestling matches or hilarious competitions to catch a pig by its slippery soaped tail. The pig was usually too quick!

Richer barons enjoyed playing chess, draughts, dice or a kind of backgammon, while they listened to musical instruments like horns, zithers and harps.

At Christmas, the baron invited the villagers into the great hall and the 'Lord of Misrule' took charge. This meant that the villagers swapped places with the baron and knights for the day, eating the best food and even being served by the noblemen!

Right *The baron and his family welcomed travelling entertainers.*

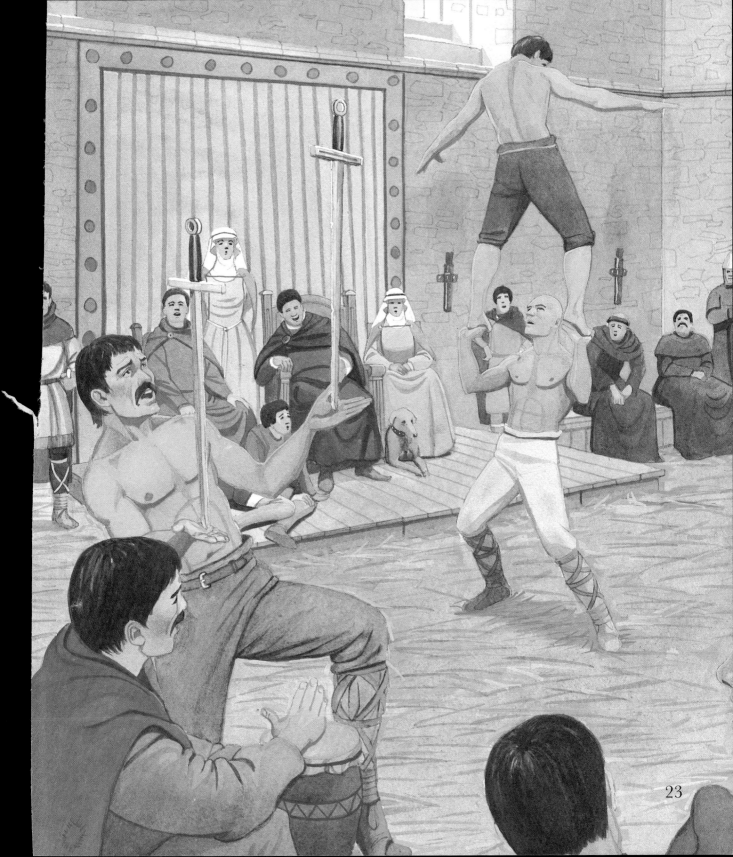

23

RELIGION AND THE CHURCH

Religion played a very important part in the baron's life. He prayed every day and celebrated many Holy Days during the year as well as Christmas, Easter and Whitsuntide.

Sunday was a day of rest and no one was allowed to work.

The church on the baron's manor was a very important building. One-tenth of the food grown on the manor

One-tenth of the food grown on the manor was given to the church. This payment was known as a 'tithe'.

Some Norman churches still stand today. This is St. Botolph's Church, Sussex.

In contrast to the simple village churches, Norman cathedrals, like this one at Winchester, were very ornate. They often took many years to complete.

was given to the village priest for the upkeep of the church.

The Church was rich and owned a great deal of land. The bishops and other churchmen were better educated than the barons and knights. Both the king and the barons tended to call on the bishops when they needed advice. Many bishops became powerful political leaders, yet it was important that the king had control over them. King Henry I, William the Conqueror's son, made the bishops swear an oath of loyalty to him before they took office.

The Normans built a great number of churches, monasteries and huge cathedrals, like those at Canterbury and Winchester. Barons often gave the land where monasteries were built. They hoped that the monks would pray for their families. Wealthy barons gave gifts of money and jewels to the Church hoping that this might save their souls from going to hell!

BARONS AND THE LAW

In Norman England the king ruled the country, but had many advisers to help him. The barons had to go to regular meetings, called 'great councils', with the king to decide the country's law.

In their manor, barons could try villagers who had done something wrong, in their own courts of law. They set up court in the great hall to hear disputes. The baron would

A villager explains his case to the baron's court.

hear such arguments as a villager accusing another of stealing his hen, or that a villager's property had been damaged in a fight. There were no police to help catch criminals, so barons sometimes recommended trial by battle to see who was in fact guilty. The accused and the accuser fought each other and whoever won was in the right! A villager who felt he had been wrongly treated could take refuge in the church where he could not be harmed.

The barons' punishments were

Above *A detail from the Domesday Book of 1086. King William requested this survey to find out the owners of every manor, along with the size of each village and its livestock.*

often very cruel. A man caught poaching might be blinded or have one hand cut off. The barons fined villagers for crimes or made them sit in the village stocks.

Men were also brought for trial at one of the country courts. Here they were tried before the sheriff and the local justice who were appointed by the king. Criminals were sometimes banished from the country and occasionally put to death.

Below *As there were no police to investigate arguments, the baron sometimes decided that trial by battle was the fairest way to settle a dispute.*

AT WAR

Norman barons were fighting men. Many were fierce and powerful, and wars often broke out between them. Barons were also called upon to fight for the king, and they had to provide their own horses, armour and weapons. They brought their supporters with them, armed with bows, arrows, staves and spears.

In England, the barons spent much of their time fighting against Hereward the Wake, a rebellious Englishman. Later, when Henry I died in 1135, the barons became involved in a nineteen-year civil war between Stephen and Matilda who both wanted the English crown. At the end of the Norman period, many barons went on crusade to the Holy Land, to try and recapture the holy cities from the fierce Saracens. The Normans also travelled south from

Normandy and established a kingdom in southern Italy, on the island of Sicily.

At war the baron wore a coat of chain mail with a hood. This was split at the front and the back so that it could be worn on horseback. The baron also wore a helmet and carried a heavy sword, a kite-shaped shield and a lance. He rode a large warhorse. This horse was specially bred to carry a rider dressed in heavy chain mail, but it could also ride at speed if necessary. Norman barons were very skilled at fighting on horseback. It was this skill which helped them defeat the English foot-soldiers at the Battle of Hastings.

Barons were often in charge of laying siege to a castle. They gave orders to batter down the gates with battering rams or to fire the stone-throwing catapaults. Sometimes the barons gave orders to prop a huge siege tower against the castle wall so soldiers could try and gain entry. All the time the defenders of the castle shot at them with long bows or dropped stones and boiling liquids down on them.

At the end of the Norman period, many barons went to fight in the crusades.

THE NORMAN LEGACY

The Norman Age ended with the death of King Stephen, in 1154. It was an age which had influenced the history of Europe for over two hundred years, and its legacy is still evident today.

The Normans built beautiful cathedrals, castles and churches, many of which still stand. They also brought with them a strong form of government, at a time when England was disorganized and weak. Many of the titles they used are familiar today, such as chancellor and treasurer.

Gradually the way of life for Norman barons changed. They married into English families, started to learn English and adopt English customs. By the middle of the twelfth century, a Norman baron was starting to think of himself as English!

The Normans Age left behind many beautiful churches and cathedrals. The choir of Canterbury Cathedral, which was finally finished in 1184, is a tribute to the French stonemason William of Sens.

GLOSSARY

Backgammon A board game for two people.

Bailiff The agent of a landlord or land-owner.

Betrothal A promise, usually made at a young age, by a boy and girl to marry each other.

Contortionist A person who entertains by twisting his or her body into strange positions.

Feudal A system of government by which land was granted in return for military or agricultural service.

Freeman A person who is not a slave or under anyone's control.

Lute A stringed instrument which is plucked rather like a guitar.

Mantle A loose wrap or cloak.

Poach To catch fish or game illegally on private property.

Portcullis An iron or wooden grating suspended in the gateway of a castle and lowered to bar the entrance.

Refuge To find shelter or protection from danger.

Saracens The name given to followers of Muhammad living in the Middle East during the Middle Age.

Serf An unfree person, especially some-one bound to the land.

Sheriff The chief officer for the crown.

Stocks A heavy wooden frame with holes in which the feet, hands or head of a wrongdoer are locked.

Tithes A payment of produce, such as grain or hay.

Venison The flesh of a deer.

Villein A peasant who worked for the lord of the manor in return for a small piece of land which he farmed as his own.

Zither A plucked musical instrument of many strings stretched over a box.

MORE BOOKS TO READ

Alfred Duggan, *Growing up with the Norman Conquest* (Faber and Faber, 1965)

Peter Lane, *Norman England* (Batsford, 1980)

Robin May, *William the Conqueror and the Normans* (Wayland, 1984)

Patrick Rooke, *The Normans* (Macdonald, 1977)

Stewart Ross, *Chaucer and the Middle Ages* (Wayland, 1985)

Peter Sauvain, *The Middle Ages* (Macmillan, 1982)

R. J. Unstead, *The Middle Ages* (A & C Black, 1974)

INDEX

Picture acknowledgements
The pictures in this book were supplied by the following: Aldus Archives 22; BBC Hulton Picture Library 12; Bodleian Library 19; Editions Alecto Limited 27 (right); Michael Holford 4, 9 (right) 30; Ronald Sheridan Picture Library 17 (right), 25 (right); TOPHAM 9 (left), 25 (left). The remaining pictures are from Wayland Picture Library.